BRILLIANCE
of DAWN

MIMI NOVIC

Aspiring Hope
Publishing

Copyright © Mimi Novic 2019

Cover images courtesy of Muni Yogeshwaran/Shutterstock © and Vecteezy.com

Cover design by EMC Design Ltd

Design and typeset by EMC Design Ltd

All rights reserved. No part of this publication may be reproduced, stored in a retrieval system, or transmitted in any form or by any means, electronic, mechanical, photocopy, recording or otherwise, without prior written permission of the copyright owner. Nor can it be circulated in any form of binding or cover other than that in which it is published and without similar condition including this condition being imposed on a subsequent purchaser.

British Library Cataloguing Publication Data.

A catalogue record for this book is available from the British Library

ISBN 978-1-9999120-4-8

Published by Aspiring Hope Publishing

In the name of God the Most Beneficent, the Most Merciful

For my beloved friend Isa, you taught me that love is the answer to all prayers and you continue to be the sublime light of my life.

For my beloved friend Muhammad, you are the one who showed me the way to the greatest love, touching my heart in all its infinite glory.

Eternally grateful to you my beautiful friends, may peace be upon you forever.

ABOUT THE AUTHOR

Mimi Novic is one of today's bestselling authors in the genre of inspirational, self-help and spiritual books.

She is one of the most highly acclaimed self-awareness teachers, having won many awards for her work.

As well as being an inspirational author and life coach in the fields of self-development and spiritual growth, she runs clinics internationally using her expertise as a therapist, complementary medical practitioner and inspirational speaker.

Through Mimi's various ground-breaking healing techniques, many have learnt to gain wellness in mind, body and spirit as well as developing positive thinking techniques to gain greater freedom to achieve a more balanced and peaceful life.

She has specialised and devised various transformational healing methods, one of the most well known and widely used ones by therapists, as well as the public, is the breathing technique, called "Healing Breath Peaceful Soul" which is a method of deep meditation and awakening through the power of breath.

Through her work as a complementary medical practitioner, therapist, voiceover artist, author and motivational speaker, she encourages everyone, from whatever walk of life they may be from, to embark upon the journey of self-discovery, in order to heal their lives. Mimi teaches seminars and workshops in alternative medicine and self-awareness, as well as complementary and holistic therapies, working around the world in clinics, retreats and on a one to one basis.

Her thought provoking writings are also available as a series of meditation albums, which beautifully harmonise her inspirations with soul enlightening music, that awaken the heart and bring peace and serenity back into our lives. An expert in her field, Mimi continues to help people find their life's purpose, through her continuing motivational work.

It is the driving force behind the passion to help people realise their true potential and transform their life so that they may become fulfilled and gain the confidence and wellbeing to achieve their lifelong ambitions and heal from within.

FOREWORD

Each one of us has an eternal symphony that forever echoes in the great mystery of our existence.

We are all lovers who with our passion and joy of the Divine thread within, intrinsically yearn the Beloved one that transcends heaven and earth.

The phenomenal power of the soul inspires the music of the heart to dance amongst the worlds of the infinite and forever trust in love of the mystical that moves us to a state of being beyond all time and space.

The ever trembling question that makes the heart strings quiver in ecstatic yearning, is how do we reach this state of grace that leads to the awakening of the Divine within us, that beckons our spirit within each breath?

The answer lies in the realisation that although we have all walked among the shadows, our inner light is like a nightingale that sings it's beautiful song, and guides us to the daybreak of hope that captures the dawn within us setting us free from all the chains of this world and propelling us into the hemispheres of the sublime, where the gentle notes of heavenly rain showers upon us to remind us of our purpose and acceptance of our real being.

It doesn't matter where we are,
It doesn't matter what surroundings we find ourselves in,
It doesn't matter where life takes us,
Nor what obstacles appear in our way,
What matters is that we never forget who we are,
And that our very presence makes everything more beautiful,
just by us being there.

There are times on our path when the hurt is too painful,
and the burden is too heavy.
But we must hang on to hope and have faith in
the power of our soul.
All we need to do is gently let go of all that gives us
pain and sadness.
Let us set ourselves free,
So, we can begin the journey towards healing
our precious hearts.

Even when we think that everything seems hopeless,
There is always one more song of hope to play,
That could turn everything around in an instant,
Never give up.

There are some people we meet at the crossroads
of our life,
Only for them to remind us, if only for a moment,
the road we need to take.
Sadly, not everyone we meet is meant to continue
the journey with us,
Yet their memory lingers forever.

$\mathcal{O}$nce in a lifetime we meet someone like no other.
They touch us so deeply, that the feeling it leaves us with is unexplainable to anyone,
They become part of us in ways we could never imagine.
It is in these moments that we can be sure that the thread of love has woven our paths together.

In everyone's eyes there is a longing to be
recognised for who we are.
Courage and love are around every corner in our life,
It is just hiding and waiting for us to be brave once again.

Never settle for anything less than you are worth. Walk away from everything that disrespects your soul.

There will be star encrusted whisperings,
　　calling for you to return,
Where eternity meets destiny once more.
　It is there that I shall wait for you,
　　in the place of timelessness,
Forever your name trembling on my lips.

The strongest feelings are the most silent.
We are all afraid of something.
We are all yearning for someone.
Yet sometimes we meet someone who invites us to live in a way like never before,
Taking us towards our greatest love.

Some people are especially sent to us,
For they are the only ones who can hear our
soul singing in the wind.
As they arrive, they ignite all our sleeping dreams.

Free yourself of other's opinions.
Don't let your voice be silenced.
Follow your inner guidance.
It knows the way.

We must not forget how powerful words are.
Their energy has the power to change, transform, destroy,
break hearts, bring sadness, give happiness, ignite love,
raise hope, heal and comfort.
Let us choose to be only with those that speak sweetly to us,
As they are the ones whose words are the balm for our heart.

Sometimes the words we never said to the ones that mattered the most, return to us in the weeping of tears.

Have courage to always speak your truth and say to another what your heart desires,

As moments never return.

There are always words that our hearts encouraged us to speak to the ones we love, and yet we missed the chance, It is these words that leave the greatest scars of regrets upon our soul.

Some days the bravest thing we can do,
Is to hold on, have hope, to keep walking,
Even just for another day.

Take your time.
Cherish every breath.
Look around you, everything has its beauty.
Give your life a meaning.
Live…Don't just exist
Find your purpose.
You are so beautiful.
If only you opened your eyes and saw the brilliance of you,
Your light would illuminate the whole world.

𝓛et us take each other by the hand to that magical place where hope resides,
Where love whispers our name,
Where the symphony of our souls plays and fills the space between us,
And infinity kisses our lips.

It doesn't matter how long we are together,
It is the beauty of the memory that it leaves etched on
our heart, that lasts for always.

All obstacles and struggles disappear,
When we end the struggle with ourselves.

We all remember the ones who touched our heart so deeply,
That our heartbeats began to dance and reminded us to
live once again.

We know nothing of this glorious soul that we are and even less about the souls that seemingly wander, yet are our companions along this way.

If we all met together in love, we would all understand each other and love each other more truly, more deeply and more genuinely.

Unless we face our fears,
We will never be able to cross the bridge to reach ourselves.

Be with the rare ones who welcome your tears,
your laughter, your sadness, your yearning, your love,
They are the real friends who grab our heart,
And throw it laughing towards the stars.

Sometimes when we think it's the end of the road,
Is when we learn to fly.

To find peace in any moment all we need to do is respect our soul.

We only struggle when we silence our heart, for then the world becomes louder,
It is then that other people's opinions start to affect us by dimming our own light.

It's what we think of as the small events, the minor details, the things that pass us by sometimes even without us noticing, That become the great things that alter our lives forever.

*O*ther's words can only affect us if we give them worth with our reaction.

By remembering that it's usually the ones who are hurting, that hurt others.

We are all searching in the darkness,

Holding out our hand ready to see each other when we see the light again,

Yet this only happens, when we learn to forgive.

We abandoned yesterday and welcomed today,
Another opportunity, another memory in the making,
another second we will never feel again.
Embrace everything in the now,
It is the way of wisdom.

𝓔 njoy every single second with those you love
and have the honour of being part of their life,
Hold them in your arms for as long as you can,
As time passes too quickly,
And memories, however beautiful, can't ever be embraced.

To be able to weep is a blessing not a weakness. Tears lighten the heart by melting the sadness we have been hiding.

Do you know what is one of the heaviest burdens to carry? Not having the courage to follow our dreams.

Remember to do everything with an abundance of love,
So that one day you will remember the beauty of every moment lived.

We all know that feeling
That once in a lifetime, trembling heartbeats,
When you know that you have found a soul that you can connect with on every single level,
That exhilarating fluttering deep inside of you,
Now go and find it.
Never settle for anything less than that.

There is no one more powerful,
Than the one who trusts their own heart.

Spend your life with people who make every second unforgettable.

Everything we do, each one we meet,
Ultimately touches us in some way and leaves its presence felt,
Maybe even without us realising, how much.

When you can be real with the way you feel,
When you are truly yourself,
When you allow your spirit freedom,
Everything around you begins to dance to
its own beautiful music.

$\mathcal{E}$ach new breath is an opportunity to try again.
Don't hide from life.
Whatever happens we are far greater than any problem that we are facing.
Look around you,
You see the sky, the flowers, the beauty, the people, absolutely everything around you,
Is showing you that you are still alive,
You are still needed here.

Sadly, sometimes those that we feel the most connected to,
By a twist of fate,
Are the ones, we are unable to spend the rest of our life with.

How we respect ourselves,
Is how we show compassion to every living being.

Every chapter of our life is written by the ink of destiny,
Let us have faith,
That our ever glorious existence will always fulfil its promise,
To return home to the One we belong to.

Be yourself in every situation, don't be affected by everything around you.
When we forget who we are is when we become heartbroken.
The moment things start to really change for the better is when we remember to make time for ourselves and respect our space.
It is one of the most important things that we can do for our whole being.
You matter and when you respect that truth,
Then whatever happens, nothing can ever disturb your peace.

The eternal circle of life begins when we are created by
the breath of our Beloved,
He who blows the wind of everlasting life beneath our wings,
Sings to our soul, so we may eternally dance in ecstatic joy.

Sometimes we forget that we were once children and within us we have all lived in magical worlds,
Where we saw everything as an adventure and showed such excitement for the smallest things.
A child's perception of life teaches us a lot.
Let's try to capture that childlike wonder again and live a little more wonderfully and beautifully.

We are never alone.
Even in the shadows our heart speaks to us, in every breath you can hear it beating,
In order to hear what it has to say, we need to allow it to speak, to allow it to guide us.
Be still, be silent, listen.
Live your truth, even if your whole being trembles,
It's a sign you are alive, and that there is still hope.

Somewhere deep inside every one of us,
Is a hidden desire, a secret longing,
A beautiful, unique connection with the Divine,
That only we know about.

We can only find our true direction,
When we let go, surrender, trust,
And allow the wind of change to carry us.

When you are brave enough to stand up for who you are and be yourself, every new step becomes an adventure.

If we meet someone with whom our heart immediately
feels a familiarity with,
We have to take the chance,
Because today is too short and tomorrow is promised
to no one.

Some people teach us everything about love in a single moment of being with them.

Some things are meant to be and some are not,
We shall never know unless we try.
The road we travel upon to find out, is usually the one that teaches us the answer.

Compassion towards another, gives us the opportunity to hear the secret of their unspoken words and listen to their message to us.

We always hold the memory of those who embraced us in the most difficult moments.

$\mathcal{E}$very now and then we must give rest to our soul.

There is an oasis that only we can reach when we follow
the river of belief.
Here we sit and bathe all our unanswered
and unrequited dreams.
If only we had the strength to submerge ourselves
into the flow of courage,
We would gain the freedom of understanding the murmur
of our long forgotten yearnings.

How wonderful it is those people that we meet by chance and invite us to live again,
The memory of them will keep the spark of joy alive forever.

Never underestimate the infinite love within you,
It has the power to transform lives.

We think that those we spend the most time with know us,
Yet some only notice our presence when we leave.
Look for the rare ones that wait for your footsteps
in the silence,
These are the one's longing to hear the echoes of your
heartbeat strum their soul.

*E*verything passes through our fingertips.
Like the sands of yesterday,
We think we have time,
Yet even the blink of our eyes fades within this second,
And the moment vanishes into the past,
Never to be seen again.

Some people arrive only when we reach a crossroads within ourselves, when decisions have to be made, when change is inevitable, but we lack the courage to embrace it.

They touch a part of us so deeply that it changes the entire direction of our life, and that exhilarating feeling of love we feel with them, is enough to guide us and give us the strength to take the right road, even if it's on our own.

𝒦eep trusting that inner voice that speaks in the silence. Your light will continue to be in your hands as long as you never give up your freedom to follow the yearning of your purpose.

Right now, in this moment we are either opening or closing the door to a new beginning, The decision is always ours.

We may not always know where we are going,
But unless we keep walking,
We will never get there to find out.

All we need is to spend time with friends that make the simple things feel extraordinary.

It can happen so very suddenly, a feeling arrives, like the
fluttering wings inside of us,
When your heart suddenly skips a beat,
When you feel an overwhelming sense of serenity, certainty
and excitement all at the same time,
That is when we need to listen closely,
As that is our heart telling us someone important
has just arrived in our life.

We all understand and hear the silent language that calls us
across the miles.
That voice of another soul calling us to meet,
At exactly the right time, the right place.
Reminding us that every meeting, is never a coincidence.

As the tears fall, the echoes hear you.
As the aching begins its yearning to be embraced,
I lay at the doorstep of your ever tender voice,
Hoping you will invite me into your arms,
So I may touch the eternal grace upon your mellow lips.

We are all conquering adversity and struggling in our own way.

By just getting up each morning and putting one foot in front of the other, we are succeeding.

Never underestimate the power of the small things that make the heart still want to keep beating.

Memories are the heart's way of sending us
kisses to caress our tears,
To remind us to keep living, to keep loving.

When we finally stop being part of what
disrespects our soul,
When we realise the worth of our being upon
the earth in the here and now,
When we accept that no one can and no one
will set us free apart from ourselves,
Only then can we begin the journey towards
fulfilling our life calling.

*D*o not be sad dear hearts, do not burden your
precious self with regrets.
Everything we do and all those we meet teaches us
a valuable lesson along the way.
Every experience is needed, nothing is a waste of time.
Each encounter is teaching us to become stronger,
wiser and to have faith in our own soul,
Only then every step we take will lead us to peace and freedom.

A grateful heart sees a glimpse of heaven in everything.

If only we had the courage to say all those unspoken words
that come to our lips,
Explored every feeling that made us feel alive,
How differently we would live.

*H*ow I yearn for you,
To hold you, to kiss you, to love you, to adore every single part of you.

Exploring your heart, soul, body, all at the same time and our spirits exploding into a million stars while we join together passionately, magically, mystically amongst the celestial.

Dancing with each other's energy beyond this world, as we take each other into another world, where we can be free to do what we wish, desire, yearn.

I will make your heart sing and your soul fly, and our music will be the music of ecstatic love that plays forever.

There are some who with one glance understand us.
There are some who without us speaking a word,
know how we feel.
There are some who remind us of the melody our heart is
singing, when we momentarily lose our way.
And then there are some who give us what we need,
without us even having to ask them.
It's these ones that hold the mirror up for us
to remember who we are.

If you want to know who are the right people
to share your life,
Look for the ones that you do not have to ask for their time,
their attention, their love.

In between the wind that carries the wings of angels,
it is there that the soul sings its song,
Waiting to be caressed by the grace of love.

When we feel mercy, compassion
and kindness from another soul,
Know that God has sent to us angels
to hold our hands together,
Reminding us that we are all part of heaven
and the great tapestry of love.

The respect people give to themselves,
Is seen in how they respect others.

*O*ne of life's greatest disappointments,
Is that we stayed too long where we were not understood.

Everything we have will one day be lost,
People, things, places, feelings.
That is the law of life.
Therefore, we must try our best to appreciate everything while it is still here.
That is the secret, not to fear the departure but to celebrate the time we have it in our lives.

Make every day count with those whose presence
means something in your life,
Too often we leave it too late to tell people how we feel.
Cherish every second,
Dance every dance with them,
Feel every touch,
Only then can our heart be in peace,
Knowing that we did all we could, while we could.

We are all connected by invisible threads.
There are special connections we feel with kindred souls.
They are the ones who strum the chords within us,
Gently guiding us towards the music of the universe.

We all fear what is inside of us and keep it locked away,
Yet this is where we will find every answer to every question.

We don't need to explain ourselves to anyone.
Those that recognise us will know and understand our words,
our tears, our gestures, our silence,
They are the ones who will welcome us with open arms,
And in whose embrace we will feel complete.

𝓔ach one of us knows our purpose,
long before we arrived here,
We have already seen the beauty of our existence.
We are just travelling through the world keeping
the promises we made to our souls.
Remember we touch every life we enter, every person we meet,
Even if it's only for a moment.

It can happen so unexpectedly that life
as quickly as it arrives, leaves.
But love, love, oh love, that never ever disappears,
It goes on eternally.

*O*ur breath, each one given to us and only us,
not knowing the number we have left.
Yet to surrender to love is to truly live beyond fear
and abide within the sanctuary of the soul.

Even if it takes a lifetime to hold their hand,
Wait for the one who will listen to your fears
and transform them into courage.

We all have moments in life where we are
left wandering what if?
It is one of the most heart wrenching questions
that we ever have to face.
Take the chance.
Take the risk.
Take the road you've never walked on.
Life is easier to live with no regrets.

Whatever happens do not stop living.
Do not give up hope.
Do not ever think it's not worth it.
It is all worth it.
And do you know why?
Because you are worth more than you could ever begin to imagine.
Your presence is needed right here right now,
That's why you are on earth.

𝒩ever for a single second mistrust your greatest friend...
Your heart,
It knows where it's taking you and where you are meant to be.

We must try to remember that everyone we meet,
Wishes, yearns, longs for, misses someone,
loves someone, has lost, has won,
And because of this, we all belong to the same
flame of love that burns within all of us.
Waiting for it to be ignited upon every prayer we whisper
for the Angels to hear in the silence of our tears
As they take it to God's door.

The weeping of your tears, the yearning for your beloved,
Outpour into the world this beautiful, glorious fragrance of
love in all its splendour.

When we show love and gratitude in every moment
for being alive,
It doesn't only change the world and the people around us,
It changes the depth of love and appreciation
we have for ourselves.

We must promise ourselves to share the real gift of our presence with the universe,
So that our life is a dedication to the beauty of our love.

The greatest adventures happen when faith leads the way.

The sacred union of lovers happens when
the spheres of the heavenly dew,
Caresses their entire being in angelic music,
Joining them in the dimensions of grace.

Never underestimate the power of your spirit.
Every single day that you get up and face what the day brings
Is a huge act of courage.

Our heart never lies,
And that is why we are at times afraid to listen it.

If you allow fear to lead your life, you will never be the one who will make your decisions where to go,
The only way to cure fear is by walking through them and shattering the illusion of its reality.

Each person we meet is waiting for us.
Our souls make the promise to see each other from long ago.
And time, takes us to that precise place for
the meeting to happen.

The unexpected meetings, moments and kisses,
Make the most unforgettable memories.

Accepting and respecting ourselves,
Is one of the greatest acts of love we can accomplish.

Every heart yearns to be opened through hope.

Our soulful whispers are guided reminders of powerful heart enriching music, that reaches out to us, gently reminding us to hold hands with the symphony of life.

We can embrace our purpose when we are in harmony with ourselves and truly enjoy the beautiful star encrusted gifts we have been given.

We all need to escape to our own peaceful sanctuary at times, our own special place.

The mystical within us yearns to be carried to the worlds where our soul can be free to fly to a moment that's suspended without time, from all that is, to all that can be.

Each passing moment is a caressing harmony of love that invites you into the space between heaven and earth.

The hidden meaning of our life is in the song our essence sings to us in each moment of us being alive.

The jewels of the heavenly treasures rain upon our soul in every living moment encouraging us to follow the road to the endless universes that will take us to forever,

With it we can touch the otherworldly existence and glimpse into infinity, by giving flight to the wings of your spirit.

As you begin to enter the gate of remembrance, every lingering word of love will resonate and echo the message of your spiritual quest.

Through the union of precious and loving words we can be entwined in the serenity of celestial music, where upon the hope of our yesterday's, we live in the hope of today's dreams, so we may fulfil the promise we were sent to earth to complete.

$\mathcal{L}$aughter with those that understand us is music for the soul,
A hug at the right moment and a kind shoulder to lean on,
Is the sprinkle of magic that keeps us walking towards joy and abundance.

We all need to be far gentler with each other,
Remembering that some people's heart's injure with far more
ease than others and dance to a quieter music.

Trust yourself, make the choice and take the risk
to be true to yourself,
It will always work out in the most beautiful of ways,
When you leave behind doubt and take the hand of courage.

Take a deep breath…Remember…Your strength is within.

Someone may touch our heart even just for a second,
But it may leave our soul stirred for a lifetime.

Everyone has their own journey and although some people's way makes no sense to you, it simply doesn't matter.

In these situations, the most loving thing you can do is allow them to follow their chosen paths.

Give yourself permission to let go, move on and do what's best for you.

Give freedom to yourself and others.

We attract all the right things and right people into our life,
When we accept and give permission to ourselves to be
completely who we are, wherever we are.

And perhaps some will never understand,
It is mostly the farewells that unite us and
last in our memory forever,
Even though destiny may separate us.

𝑂f all the greatest beginnings and endings in a love story,
It is the last goodbye that leaves its imprint on us forever.

Let us be the few who at least try to be brave and make a change in a world which is ever losing courage.

It is not in our words but in our sighs that the most important feelings are felt.

$\mathcal{I}$ look at the space of emptiness, the memory
of your perfume only fragrances the gentle breeze
now of where you once stood.

The light of my being flickers only so that it may see you once
more and to behold a single drop of grace.

Yet the emptiness can never be filled, as you my love
have left the sphere of this world and as I close my eyes,
I wish to be taken home, for I know there you will wait for me,
for a lifetime or more.

Among the ruins of the past,
There is always the hope of today.

There are feelings that are unpronounceable in words,
Only the soul can interpret them.

If no one wants to accompany you,
Have courage, still go,
You will find your companions along the road.

We are all particles of lingering stardust swirling amongst the mists of time,
Joining each other in the ever flowing ocean of forever,
Embracing the twilight and holding our breath hoping that we entwine in the morning dew.

Adore the people who appear on your way and make you forget where you were going,
These enlightened ones have the power to change your journey, in the unforgettable brilliance of a single moment.

𝒪nly when we recognise the worth of loving ourselves,
Will we be able to learn to forget all those people that did not bring us closer to love.

What is it to Live?

It is to vibrate in your own energy and cause ripples in the hearts you meet.

It is to be free to feel and free to love in every new opportunity.

It is to savour every new experience and for everything that comes along, accept it as a discovery.

It is to observe and to overcome every difficulty without it becoming part of you.

It is to give thanks and to accept and to understand that our time is the only one thing we are all given individually, to realise fully our being.

How we spend each one of those precious seconds,

Is how we are deciding to live our life.

There are moments, and then there are other moments,
And then there are unspeakable moments,
That only we will always live alone in.
Silently, remembering them forever.

Make love be the prayer you say every day.

𝓛et us forgive ourselves,
For not realising some things sooner.

Each new breath gives us another glorious moment to look within ourselves and to see who we are. Only then can we help others reach the shores to themselves.

Don't stand still.
Don't wait for anyone.
Who is meant to be your companion will take your hand.
The Divine hand has prepared everything for you,
Live now…not for yesterday, not for tomorrow,
Today is the only day we have to touch the beauty of forever.

Every step you make takes you to an unpredictable destination and that's what makes it fascinatingly beautiful. Always leave space for the unimaginable, exciting and awe inspiring to enter your life.

𝓛ife is so short, even less than the blink of an eye.
Kiss slowly,
Laugh loudly,
Forgive quickly,
Try something new every day,
Hope without end,
Dance passionately,
Love intensely,
Never miss a chance to be free to enjoy
the magic of who you are.

www.ingramcontent.com/pod-product-compliance
Lightning Source LLC
Chambersburg PA
CBHW060400080526
44583CB00012B/409